SENSORY LIKE YOU

A book for kids with SPD by adults with SPD

RacHeL S. ScHNeider, M.A., MHC
& KeLLy DiLLoN

Sensory Like You

All marketing and publishing rights guaranteed to and reserved by:

800-489-0727
www.sensoryworld.com
info@sensoryworld.com

ISBN: 978-1935567707

Dedications

For my baby-girl-to-be. I'm not sure who you're destined to become quite yet, but I promise you I'll love and support you all the way. —R.S.

For my favorite little gentlemen, Liam and Logan —K.D.

Think of your favorite grown-up.

Maybe it's your mom or dad, your big silly brother or sister, your quiet cousin, the grandma who hugs you tightly, the teacher who wears colorful shirts, or even your next-door neighbor who loves to bake cookies. What do grown-ups do? They work hard at their jobs, take care of the house and many other things. They have pets and hobbies. They have families and friends. They like to have fun!

Well, we're grown-ups too . . . and we're sensory like you.

Kelly's sensory like you. She's an artist who loves making people laugh through her beautifully funny drawings. Kelly always draws herself wearing her owl hat because it makes her feel comfortable.

Rachel's also sensory like you. She's a writer who loves creating stories about how she's feeling inside to help other people. Rachel wears glasses with blue lenses that allow her see the world around her more easily.

Our senses help us figure out the world around us. We know that a baby is hungry or sleepy because we hear it crying. We know to cross the street because we see the light turn green. We can tell when we're hungry because we feel and/or hear our stomachs growling.

TOUCHING

(WITH your HaNds or SKiN)

TASTING

(WiTH your MoUTH and tonGUe)

SEEING

(WitH your eyeS)

HEARING

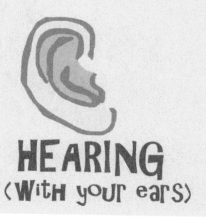

(WiTH your earS)

SMELLING

(WiTH your NoSe)

Did you know that you have eight senses? You might know the first five senses already:

1. Seeing (with your eyes)
2. Hearing (with your ears)
3. Touching (with your hands or skin)
4. Tasting (with your mouth and tongue)
5. Smelling (with your nose)

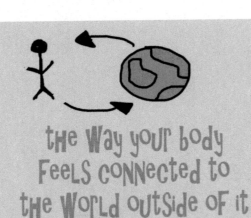

the Way your body
FeeLS coNNected to
the World outSide of it

BALANCE

the Way your orgaNS,
LiKe your StoMacH
aNd Heart,
FeeL iNSide your body

You have three more senses that you might not know. They're senses that relate to the whole body:

1. Balance
2. The way your organs, like your stomach and heart, feel inside of your body
3. The way your body feels connected to the world outside of it

How do you feel when things are very bright, loud, smelly, strong-tasting, crunchy, moving, or touching your skin? Do you feel happy and want more? Do you feel scared and want to run away? Do you not even notice these things?

Well, guess what? What you feel is not in your imagination. You're not dreaming how you're feeling. You're not making anything up.
We feel the same things too because we're sensory like you.

These feelings have a name. It's called Sensory Processing Disorder, but you can call it SPD for short.

Having SPD is like living with a tiny traffic jam in your brain. All of those bright, loud, smelly, strong-tasting, crunchy, moving, and skin-touching things are like the cars. They all drive into your brain at once, which feels like too much to handle.

We know that because of your SPD, you feel different sometimes. We feel different too because we're sensory like you. When we feel different, we like to remember lots of people live in the world. Some people are tall and some are short. Some have light skin and some have dark skin. Some have brown eyes and some have blue eyes. Some have big feet and some have small feet. Some even have different brains.

Some brains are made in a way that make us especially sensitive to the same things that make you sensitive – like when the light is too bright at school, or you can't stop hugging your mom. Our brains are just like yours! You have SPD, and we do too, because we're sensory like you.

It's totally okay to be different. Different doesn't mean good or bad. It just means that there is no one way for things to be in this world. How boring would life be if we were all the same? What if everything around you was the color green? Imagine green people and a green sky. Different people with different experiences bring fun and new ideas into our lives to keep things interesting.

We like to think that people with SPD have some very special powers. Because we're so sensitive, we sometimes notice things that other people don't even notice. Have you ever realized that a friend was sad before they started to cry? Or did you ever think that someone needed you to help them before they even asked for your help?

We also know how tough it can be to have SPD. Remember, it's tough for us too because we're sensory like you. Our superpowers are almost too super sometimes! We can be so sensitive that we drink in all of the color, light, energy, and movement around us until we feel like we're going to explode. We can also be so hungry for color, light, energy, and movement that we never feel like we can get enough.

We know that it's no fun to be uncomfortable. However, remember, our brains don't always tell us the truth about sounds, sights, tastes, touches, smells, or movements. Sometimes, we get more scared than we need to be because our brains are telling us to worry. The good news is that we are safe in our bodies, even when our bodies are telling us that we're not safe. In your skin, you are safe in this world. We promise! We're safe too because we're sensory like you.

One of the things that will help teach your brain how to feel safer is called Occupational Therapy, or OT for short. OT is so much fun! You'll get to play games and learn how to feel better at home, school, and everywhere in between. Sometimes you'll even be given new toys or tools that you can use to make yourself feel better.

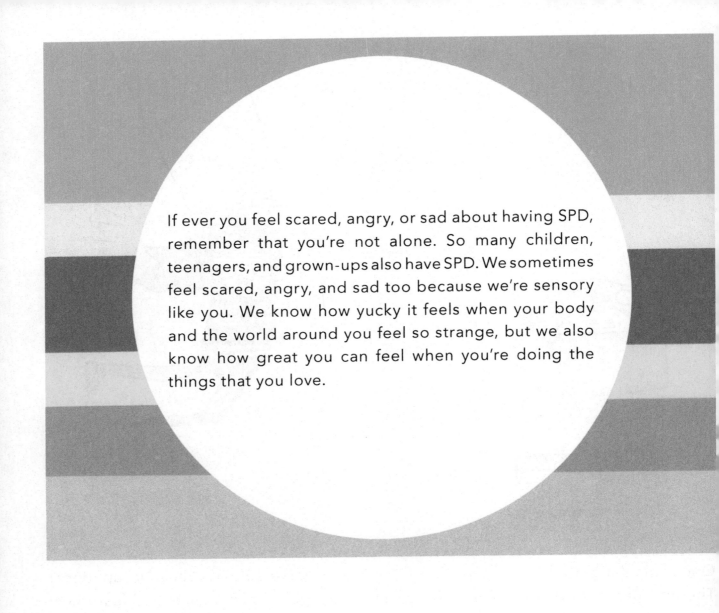

If ever you feel scared, angry, or sad about having SPD, remember that you're not alone. So many children, teenagers, and grown-ups also have SPD. We sometimes feel scared, angry, and sad too because we're sensory like you. We know how yucky it feels when your body and the world around you feel so strange, but we also know how great you can feel when you're doing the things that you love.

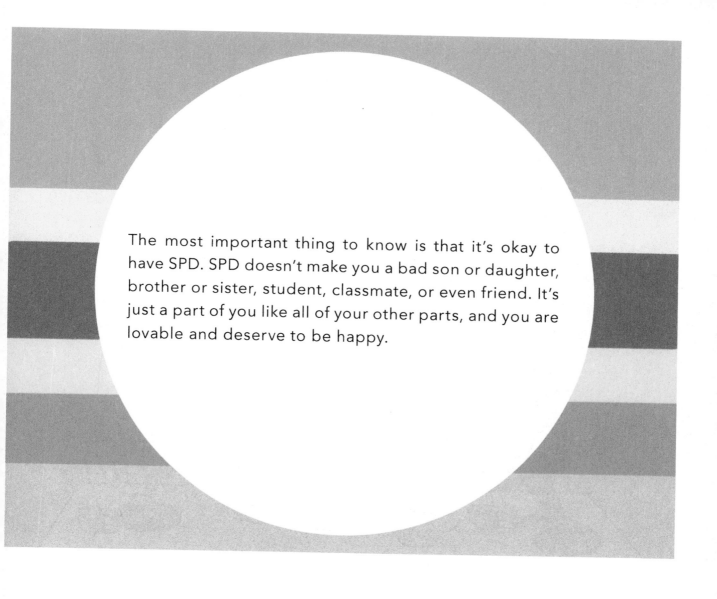

The most important thing to know is that it's okay to have SPD. SPD doesn't make you a bad son or daughter, brother or sister, student, classmate, or even friend. It's just a part of you like all of your other parts, and you are lovable and deserve to be happy.

Sometimes, we like to imagine that we're having our own little tea party for SPD. We imagine leaving one empty chair for SPD and ask it to join us at our table. When it sits down, we give it a cupcake and a big smile. We can't make SPD go away, so we make room for it in our minds instead. We welcome it over. We even make friends with it.

Think of your favorite grown-up again. What do grown-ups do? They work hard at their jobs, take care of the house and many other things. They have pets and hobbies. They have families and friends. They like to have fun! Someday, you'll be a grown-up. You'll laugh, play, work, and love . . . and you'll have SPD too. We do. We're grown-ups, and we're sensory like you.

AUTHOR

Rachel S. Schneider, M.A., MHC is the author of Making Sense: A Guide to Sensory Issues, which was published by Sensory World in February 2016. As a writer, mental health counselor, delayed-diagnosis SPD adult, and pillar of the adult SPD community, Rachel writes the popular sensory blog - Coming to My Senses, and authored the hit articles "The Neurotypicals' Guide to Adults with Sensory Processing Disorder" and "What Everyone Should Know About Sensory Processing Disorder." Rachel lives in New York City with her husband and handler, Josh.

ILLUSTRATOR

Kelly Dillon is a writer and illustrator based in the Hudson Valley. She chronicles her life with Sensory Processing Disorder on the illustrated blog, Eating off Plastic.

Also by Rachel S. Schneider

Our senses! Thanks to them, our brains are constantly flooded with information about the world around us. What may surprise you is that we're not all wired the same way, and some of us are unable to understand exactly what we're sensing. People with Sensory Processing Disorder (SPD), a newly identified neurological condition, as well as those with an Autism Spectrum Disorder (ASD), are frequently misunderstood by others when they over- or under-react to sounds, sights, smells, tastes, touch, movement, balance, and feelings within their bodies.

Price: $14.95

Also available at:

CPSIA information can be obtained
at www.ICGtesting.com
Printed in the USA
BVOW07s2325281116
468665BV00020B/1/P